Sullivan Publishing, LLC
Chicago, IL
www.sullybaby.com

Copyright ©2003 **Mark Joseph Sullivan**

Printed in the United States of America

10 9 8 7 6 5 4 3 2 1

Library of Congress Control Number: 2003094947

ISBN 0-9720318-1-2

Sully Baby's™

GUIDE TO

URBAN

LIVING

Mark Sullivan

For the wonderfully diverse multitudes that make the city so special.

Thanks to

Mark Ostrowski
Rob Porazinski
Sarah Korhonan
Sean Dwyer

Special thanks to Amanda Curtis

INTRODUCTION

When cultural capitals of the world are listed, you will find cities; great cities from London to Budapest, from Paris to Chicago. It is rare that a suburb will pop up on the list, although occasionally one finds Cicero, Illinois, birthplace of the great Roman statesman. While the city can provide an electrifying cultural atmosphere with never ending possibilities, it can also be difficult to manage. Welcome to Sully Baby's Guide to Urban Living, the consummate guide to city life. Everything from how to deal with noisy neighbors to finding authentic ethnic food, it's all here. Sully Baby combines useful information with a healthy dose of humor to make your reading both productive and entertaining. I sincerely hope you enjoy Sully Baby's Guide to Urban Living. And remember, while it's not easy to live in the city, life could be worse. You could be stuck in the suburbs.

Sully Baby

Table of Contents

Section 1: Getting Around

Section 2: Making it Through

Section 3: Having Some Fun

Section 1
Getting Around

Chapter 1

Public Transportation

You've waited 30 minutes in the pouring rain for a bus. As it draws near, you realize the driver has no intention of stopping. But he **will** splash through the gigantic puddle directly in front of you. Welcome to public transportation.

Objective 1: Stop a Bus Whose Driver Appears Unwilling to Stop

Bus drivers choose not to stop for passengers for two reasons: 1) the bus is overcrowded, and 2) sadistic pleasure.

Method A - Look at the driver with an expression of desperation

This method is frequently successful with compassionate drivers who think their bus just can't fit one more passenger. Communicating an aura of desperation, you may elicit enough sympathy for the driver to stop. Be prepared if the bus passes; have your middle finger ready for immediate action.

Method B - Unrelenting blockade

Thrust your arm in front of the bus' path and look directly into the eyes of the driver while displaying an expression of unrelenting determination. Because of the inherent danger, this method is only recommended for persons already equipped with a quick-release prosthetic arm.

Objective 2: Avoid Having an Undesirable Rider Sit Next to You

Undesirable riders include (but are not limited to) those who smell, those who sweat profusely, those who cough and sneeze, those who require more than one full seat, those who want to chat, and those who interfere with your personal space.

Method A - Sit down next to a desirable rider
It is axiomatic that if one sits next to a desirable rider, one won't get stuck next to an undesirable rider. But remember, that good looker with gorgeous eyes and a great suit may have a nasty case of body odor.

Method B - Remain standing
You may like sitting at a window seat, but its appeal diminishes when a Jehovah's Witness sits next to you and insists on handing out the latest issue of *Watchtower*. By standing, one is in the best position to flee locational crises.

Method C - Behave undesirably to undesirable riders
It's a rare occurrence when anyone will get within 5 feet of you as you're loudly humming the theme to *Rocky* while shadowboxing in the aisle. Don't worry, you won't get kicked off the bus. Bus drivers ignore people like you.

Objective 3: Wage a Battle Against Cell Phone Users

If cell phone users were as important as they thought, they wouldn't be taking public transit.

Method A - Invade the cell phone user's personal space
Since they're in your face, get in their's.

Method B - Read aloud
Instead of silently reading your newspaper or book, begin to read it aloud. You'll improve your public speaking skills and disturb the cell phone offender.

Method C - Verbal retaliation
Look at the person and state, "Excuse me. Please stop talking on your cell phone. I'm afraid it makes you look like an ass." This method is especially applicable toward hands-free cell phone users.

Objective 4: Board a Crowded Train During Rush Hour

During rush hour, subway and elevated trains are crowded, run sporadically, and have the most distressed passengers. It's within this environment that one must use ingenuity to achieve passage.

Method A - Push your way on

Aggressive personalities enjoy pushing their way in front of other waiting passengers and shoving themselves onto a crowded train. The pleasure of this method is increased by waving to people on the platform as the train moves away with you on board.

Method B - Pretend you're mentally unstable

Twitch nervously and shout unexplainable rants at nearby passengers. You'll part the crowd faster than Moses parted the Red Sea.

Method C - Stand by the bad musician

The guy playing a Van Halen drum solo on a bucket may seem like a nuisance; however, during rush hour, he may be your best ally in the battle to board the train. Anyone who can bear to be next to him deserves first shot when the doors open.

Special Section
Grieving

Denial, anger, bargaining, depression, and acceptance. Rumor has it that Dr. Elisabeth Kubler-Ross developed the five stages of grief after missing a train.

DENIAL
No matter how fast you run after the bus, or how fast you tackle the stairs to the subway, the bus is long gone and your train's left the station. Deal with it so you can move on to Sully Baby's favorite stage, anger.

ANGER
The world's against you. Screaming obscenities and punting your briefcase 40 feet is a good way to vent, and a football scout may notice your excellent form.

BARGAINING
You've already exceeded your monthly quota of requests to God. Move on to depression.

DEPRESSION
Somebody has to suffer for your shortcomings; it might as well be you.

ACCEPTANCE
Sully Baby has no experience with this stage and is therefore unable to comment.

Chapter 2
Taxis

It's great to be in a place where thousands of taxis roam the streets. Too bad they all disappear when you need one.

Objective 1: Catch a Taxi During Rush Hour

For those who subscribe to blatant optimism, it may be worth attempting to catch a taxi during rush hour.

Method A - Steal someone's cab

That guy on crutches doesn't deserve that cab anymore than you. Feign ignorance, get in, close the door, and be off.

Method B - Find a taxi drop-off

If you happen to be near a commuter train station on the way home, you'll find taxi after taxi dropping off fleeing suburbanites rushing to their trains. You'll get a cab, but the driver may have his boxers in a bunch. He probably just got stiffed on a tip.

Method C - Wait until rush hour is over

It's virtually impossible to catch a taxi during rush hour. If you beat the odds, you'll be stuck in traffic anyway. You might as well be late to work. You've been passed up for a promotion three years running anyway.

Objective 2: Catch a Taxi when it's Raining

The ease of rush hour tactics is gone when it rains. Wet people are mean people, hence one must either pass on the objective or resort to guerrilla warfare.

Method A - Steal someone's cab

It's not as easy to steal someone's cab when it's raining. An attempt may result in serious conflict. The best approach is going on a pseudo-psychotic offensive. Wait until a person is about to enter a cab and run up screaming, "That's my cab you bastard!" The shock of the unsuspecting victim will usually last long enough to enter the cab and escape.

Method B - Wave a twenty dollar bill in the air

In the unlikely event a vacant taxi spots you, they will go directly to you, passing by all of the other desperate people waving fives. The driver doesn't have to know that you have no intention of giving him the twenty.

Method C - Wait the rain out

When it's raining, the probability of getting one's newly cleaned clothes soaked from a taxi going through a large puddle at high speed is significantly greater than actually catching a cab. Sometimes it's better to just give up.

Objective 3: Find an Aggressive Taxi Driver

Not all taxi drivers are created equal. For those in a hurry, it's essential to secure an aggressive driver.

Method A - Go with the driver who cuts off another taxi to get your fare

During off-peak times, it's common to have two cabbies notice your uplifted arm. Etiquette would suggest that you take the taxi which first responds. But forget etiquette and take the taxi that slams on the breaks, makes a screeching U-turn across four lanes of traffic, and cuts in front of the first cab on the scene.

Method B - Look for the cab with the most dents

A severely beaten taxi is an excellent indication of the personality of its driver. Remember to wear your seatbelt.

Objective 4: Irritate a Taxi Driver

The sign located on the partition rubbing against your knee states that drivers must be courteous to passengers, and passengers must be courteous to drivers. Fortunately, some tourist covered it over with a *Don't Mess with Texas!* bumper sticker.

Method A - Tell the driver he's going too fast

Many passengers become uncomfortable at speeds in excess of 85 miles per hour. A surefire way to irritate the racing driver is to tell him to slow down. However, if you really want him to slow down, you'll have to say you're getting car sick and are about to heave.

Method B - Mumble insults

In an audible tone, mumble insults every time the driver makes an incompetent move. This passive-aggressive method is particularly irritating to drivers because you can accuse them of eavesdropping if they respond.

Method C - Proclaim, "Nice move asshole!"

Cabbies generally become irritated when their driving is sarcastically insulted and they are referred to as an unpleasant bodily orifice. This provocative method should only be used if there are other taxis readily available.

Special Section

The Great Urban Taxicab Myth

Legend has it that one may call a taxicab company and procure a cab in a timely manner. This is only a myth which is promulgated by taxicab companies having listed phone numbers. Some companies even have operators that promise to dispatch a taxi to your requested location. If a taxi ever arrives through such a process, consider it a coincidence.

Special Section

Respect your Driver's Intellect

If one would like to have an intellectual conversation, particularly with regard to politics, taxi drivers are a good choice. Cabbies may be horrible drivers and inept navigators, but their intellectual acumen is outstanding. This is bolstered by the diversity of cultures from which they originate and encounter as well as the fact that the average taxi driver listens to fourteen hours of National Public Radio a day.

Chapter 3
Walking

Frequently overlooked by residents and visitors, often the quickest and most cost-effective means of transportation from point A to point B is by foot. Unfortunately, cars, people and buildings can get in the way.

Objective 1: Navigate Through the Masses Crowding the Sidewalk

As if it weren't enough trying to get by the two business people that have stopped to chat in the middle of the sidewalk, you also have to contend with tourists, shoppers, protesters, and high schoolers on "Senior Ditch Day."

Method A - Walk confidently

Confidence works wonders in many aspects of life, and walking is no exception. A confident attitude will cause others to part and, if not, you can have some really decent collisions.

Method B - Slalom

If you ever wondered if there was a practical application of early generation video games, here it is. Walk at one's normal pace, but in a slaloming pattern that avoids anyone in front of you. Simply look for the clearest path and take it.

Method C - Loudly proclaim, "Excuse me!"

While the expression "excuse me" is typically associated with a polite gesture, this is not the case when trying to make progress while walking on an overcrowded sidewalk. In such a situation the expression "excuse me" is simply a socially acceptable saying, "OUT OF MY WAY, ASSHOLE!"

Objective 2: Face an Onslaught of Suburban Commuters

It's always best to avoid a charging herd of cattle; however, sometimes it's necessary to go up against it. When facing suburbanites coming from or going to the train station, these patented methods are recommended.

Method A - Briefcase Block

Shields were invented for a reason. You may not have crested armor, but the briefcase you're holding isn't a bad substitute. Hold it in front of you and defend yourself.

Method B - Umbrella Flail

Take a closed umbrella (ideally, not a folding umbrella; length does matter) and wave it in front of you. Joyously erupt in the occasional "En Garde!"

Method C - Locomotive

Aggressive counter-directionalists and train enthusiasts may choose the locomotive. Put your arms in front of you like the cow catcher on an old steam locomotive. Loudly proclaim, "Toot! Toot!" and plow ahead.

Objective 3: Avoid Being Hit by a Moving Vehicle

Vehicles lurk in the dark recesses of the city's mean streets. When you least expect it, they pounce on their unsuspecting prey like a creature of the night.

Method A - Look both ways before you cross the street

A crossing guard isn't there to help you anymore. Look both ways and beware of cars shooting out from alleys, garages, driveways, and any other blind spots.

Method B - Jump over the moving vehicle

Although it looks easy in the movies, don't be fooled. This stunt is virtually impossible and the probability of a successful vault goes down dramatically when facing sport-utility vehicles, trucks and buses. Please note that attempting to jump over a Geo Metro may cause extensive body damage to the vehicle.

Method C - Wear protective clothing

Accessorize your business suit with hockey pads, a motorcycle helmet, and a bright orange hunting jacket. Drivers (as well as pedestrians) will avoid you; and in the unlikely event of impact, injury will be mitigated.

Special Section

Undesirable Substances

Like any environment, the city is filled with substances that are unpleasant to step into: vomit, dog turds, dog urine, horse apples, horse urine, and mucus (particularly that which is shaded green or yellow).

VOMIT

Vomit is most commonly found in areas with a high density of drinking establishments. Fortunately, taverns are generally concentrated within specific areas. Particular caution should be taken within a four block radius of these areas, particularly on Saturday and Sunday mornings.

DOG TURDS

Dog ownership ethics and recent improvements in municipal laws have dramatically reduced the amount of solid dog waste found in urban areas. Unfortunately, urban parks seem to be exempt. Nothing can do more to ruin a romantic walk or deflate the glee of children at play than stepping into dog doo. When on a romantic walk, stick to walkways and paths. When out with the kids, a few minutes of reconnaissance can save hours of frustration.

DOG URINE

Dog urine is difficult to identify. The good news is that it's not the end of the world if you step into it, as long as you're not going directly into your place of residence. If you happen to step into dog urine, walk outside for a while, then walk into a public area with a carpet that has a thicker pile than the one at home.

HORSE APPLES For reasons that range from an uninformed romanticism of the horse-and-carriage to the practicality of crowd control for police forces, the horse has found an unlikely resurgence in the urban setting. Most municipalities, while encouraging increased equine activity, require sacks be placed under horse posteriors. But these bags aren't used on police horses, so bring your boots to summer fest.

HORSE URINE Don't ignore the risk of encountering horse urine. Don't think "stepping into;" think "splashed by." The powerful force of horse urination is magnified by the concrete landing surface. On windy days, a fine mist may be observed as far as thirty feet away. Avoid the horse but enjoy the sight of that newly waxed Jaguar with the elegantly dressed couple inside getting spritzed.

MUCUS If you watch someone for long enough, they will spit. Their mucus poses a threat to your white K-Swiss that look so fresh and so clean. While it is disgusting to look down in search of mucus, the alternative is much worse.

Chapter 4
Driving

If you're wondering how to coexist with the Hummer that just took out the Kia to your left, this chapter's for you. It won't turn the experience into a Sunday drive, but it may reduce the damage to your front quarter panel.

Objective 1: Avoid Traffic Congestion

A jerk in a BMW just went through a yellow light only to be stopped mid-intersection by traffic. Now you're blocked. Do you use your '81 Monte Carlo as a battering ram or continue to patiently wait? Avoid tough choices. Avoid traffic.

Method A - Don't drive

Those who don't drive will find they are rarely caught in traffic.

Method B - Drive between 2 a.m. and 5 a.m.

Traffic flow is exceptional, but if you're cruising the strip between these hours, you're either a cop or a loser.

Method C - Take circuitous routes

Everyone thinks they know a way around a traffic jam and everyone is generally wrong. If you find a back road to avoid traffic, you're no longer in the city. Suck it up and deal with the gridlock.

Objective 2: Get Around a Bus

Slow city traffic can get even slower if you find yourself behind a bus. Frustration may diminish as the toxic bus fumes take hold, but living in the clouds isn't where it's at.

Method A - *Stay out of the right lane*
The best way to avoid buses is to avoid the right lane unless you're turning. You'll not only avoid the bus, but also the car waiting to turn right while mom helps junior cross the street on his trike.

Method B - *The Swerving Rocky*
Taking a right turn in front of a bus can be tricky, not to mention, illegal. The law will be the least of your problems. Thirty-two standing passengers who fell down when the bus slammed on the brakes have just put a hex on you.

Method C - *The Pass*
In theory, a bus should move to the right at any bus stop thereby giving you an opportunity to pass. Theory is not always followed by practice. Hit the blinker and head left.

Method D - *Use streets without bus service*
This seems like a good idea, but it's better to be behind a bus that makes slow progress than to be stuck behind a double-parked U-Haul on a narrow one-way street.

Objective 3: Pick the Right Vehicle to Drive

It's not as simple as going to the showroom and picking a paint color. You're in the city and you need to consider the bulletproof glass option.

Method A - Drive an SUV

There are practical applications of an SUV in the city. SUV's won't implode when they hit a pot hole, they won't get run over by another SUV, and they offer seating height without the embarrassment of driving a minivan. Don't get carried away though. The "Monster Trucks Rule" calendar thrown in by the dealer should be disposed of immediately.

Method B - Drive a beater

You may not get style points for driving an '86 Ford Tempo with 136,000 miles on the odometer, but when you hit a pothole and drop the transmission, you can just walk away. The driver in a new Mercedes has to wait for a tow.

Method C - Straddle your ride

The new urban rage in America is the scooter. Fuel efficient, maneuverable and easy to park, these conveyances have been popular in Europe for decades. Ride a Vespa and be hip, but wear a helmet because 4-inch tires don't stand up well to the 2x4 that just fell off the roof of that Audi pulling out of Home Depot.

Special Section

Open Your Car Door Responsibly

If you're unfamiliar with the term of "dooring," it's the act of throwing open your car door, directly into the chosen path of an unsuspecting biker pedaling at 40 mph. Although the concept sounds funny, it's actually quite painful and may leave a huge dent in your door. Be sure to open your door responsibly.

Chapter 5
Parking

Many have heard the legend of the urban parking space. The legend's genesis is unknown, yet continues to be passed down through the generations.

Objective 1: Avoid Parking Problems

After living in an urban area for a period of time, one learns that the parking nightmare never goes away. The only way to sleep easy is to follow these methods.

Method A - Don't buy a car

If you don't have a car to park, you won't have a parking problem.

Method B - If you own a car, sell it

Same as above, but you'll have enough extra spending money to upgrade the Schwinn you inherited from your grandmother.

Method C - Take Greyhound

If you're visiting a city, it's a mistake to drive a car and face parking problems. Choose Greyhound and hang with the Amish and punk rockers.

Objective 2: Find Street Parking

Automobiles driven by hopeful or desperate drivers are frequently spotted going around the same block for days searching for a parking space. Finding street parking is generally a fruitless endeavor; but if you must, the following will assist you in your misguided adventure.

Method A - *Park prior to a parking restriction time lapsing*
Put on the blinkers and don't leave the vehicle until the legal parking time. Don't mind the cop writing a ticket and placing it on your window. It's cheaper than the garage down the street.

Method B - *Arrive earlier than any normal human being would find reasonable*
If you're going downtown to work and wish to find metered parking, arrive before 5:00 a.m. A high probability exists that you'll find a space; one that you'll no longer need after being fired for sleeping on the job.

Method C - *Become an art major*
Art majors have unlimited access and proper know-how to forge parking permit stickers. Ironically, art majors can't afford a car. Besides, counterfeiting is wrong.

Objective 3: Find Reasonably Priced Off-Street Parking

If one finds it necessary to park in a garage, get ready for sticker shock. Even frequent parkers are astonished at the ever-increasing cost of parking within urban areas. Expect to pay well in excess of $20 for a few hours of parking. But don't rush, the first half-hour is $19.50.

Method A - Validated parking

Stores and restaurants are beginning to catch on that parkers may have purchased a $2.00 air freshener or a $3.00 cup of cappuccino to reduce the cost of parking by $10.00, but there are still some that will validate for a minimal purchase. Opt for the air freshener; the burritos were a bad call tonight.

Method B - Go to a surface lot

Surface lots are over-crowded, poorly located and filled with pot holes. But many select these lots to reduce their parking cost by as much as 4% per day, which means if you do it 25 days in a row you've reduced parking costs by 100% and you're parking for free. Right?

Method C - Go to a city garage

City owned garages are cheaper than privately owned garages, but you get what you pay for. Don't park under that chunk of concrete dangling from the ceiling.

Objective 4: Park in a "Full" Garage

It's not uncommon to find oneself in a situation where there are no apparent available parking spaces; but just as there is no such thing as a hotel without an available room or a restaurant without a table, there is no parking lot without a space. The key is knowing how to get it.

Method A - Drive up to see if a ticket spits out of the machine and the gate goes up

Garage managers often turn on the "garage full" sign prior to a garage filling up to accommodate monthly parkers. Some ticket machines can't disengage, so you'll be able to enter and park. If not, you'll be stuck at the gate and have the satisfaction of creating an incredible traffic jam of irritated monthly parkers.

Method B - If the garage has valet parking, simply give the attendant incentive compensation

If an executive can receive a bonus for squeezing a little more profit from a business, why shouldn't an attendant receive a bonus for creating a parking space from nothing. Surely, this is capitalism at its finest.

29

Special Section

Tow Zones

DO NOT PARK IN A TOW ZONE

Don't park in a tow zone, not even for a minute, not even with your flashers on, not for any reason. Most urban areas now have covert surveillance systems with instant notification to incredibly rude tow truck drivers that will arrive within 45 seconds after you walk away. The car will be gone within another 60-90 seconds. No civilian has yet determined the technology behind the surveillance systems; but due to the rapid response time, scientists are confident that such a system exists.

PUBLIC TOWING If your car is towed by a municipality, you'll not only pay the towing charge and taxi fare to the lot, but also a stiff fine for the parking ticket received. Incidentally, the city lot officer guarding your car won't believe you when you claim the car was more than 15 feet from the hydrant when it was towed.

PRIVATE TOWING While private towing doesn't come with the cost of a parking ticket, you can be assured that a huge orange sticker will be attached to your driver's side window with industrial strength glue, you'll have to take a taxi to a remote lot on the outskirts of the city, and 22 rabid dogs will greet you. Don't even think about asking if they take checks.

Chapter 6
Airports

Nothing against Cheeseheads, but the air industry is in a sorry state when Milwaukee has the best airport in the United States. As a general rule, if your destination is within 1,200 miles, it's better to drive.

Objective 1: Get to the Airport

Whatever you do, DON'T DRIVE. Cars filling airport lots are parked by those who think it's efficient to park two miles away from the airport, wait twenty minutes for transportation to the terminal, and pay $30 a day for the thrill of returning to discover their car has been stolen.

Method A - Hail a taxi

Despite leaving six hours early, weather or traffic will ruin any chance of catching your flight. There are better ways to spend time than sitting in traffic watching the meter eat away your kid's college fund.

Method B - Hail a friend

If you ask a friend to drive you to or from the airport, you'll have one less friend. No one is happy to see you after they've made forty-seven loops of the terminal.

Method C - Take public transportation

In many urban areas, this is arguably the only way to travel to and from airports. It's fast, convenient and cheap. As an added bonus, you can wave at the losers stuck in traffic as your train rushes by.

Method D - Take a limo

You may get stuck in traffic, but limos are definitely sexier than public transit. And if you want some bubbly, you can pour it into a glass rather than sucking a "40" from a brown paper bag.

Objective 2: Check In in Less than Two Hours

The six-thousand passengers waiting in line is not an illusion. The sea of vehicles that were in front of you on the expressway have just dropped off passengers that are now in front of you at check in.

Method A - Check in curbside

The optimal method of checking in is to pay a slight fee to have redcaps check your bags curbside and handle the boarding pass process. The fee is typically about $1 per bag, but it's a good idea to pay a minimum of $2 per bag. Your bags will receive priority treatment, meaning they have a 50% chance of getting on the plane.

Method B - Go first class

Just when you thought first class wasn't worth the 500% premium over coach, you find out that there's a separate check in line. So there is more to first class than having passengers flying coach snarl at you as they board, a wider seat to plant your fat ass, and pseudo-gourmet food that gives you instant diarrhea.

Method C - Join an airline club

Airline clubs promise a more peaceful environment in which to check in. When going through the sliding glass doors (frosted to keep the riff-raff from peeking in), one enters a world with upholstered seats, berber carpeting, wood paneling and a pleasant attendant to check you in.

Objective 3: Make a Connection

There's more to making a connection at a large airport than deplaning and walking a few feet to the next gate. You'll have to be an expert navigator, stay in excellent condition, and slalom through the teeming masses.

Method A - Use the same airline

If you use the same airline, it's a safe bet that your connecting flight is less than a half-mile away. You'll also have a better chance at cooperation when you miss your connecting flight.

Method B - Schedule 6 hours between connecting flights

It will only take two hours to walk to the connecting gate, but your initial flight will probably be 2½ hours late and it will take 1½ hours to read *Better Homes & Gardens* cover to cover at the newsstand.

Method C - Develop a limp

For some reason, airlines think it's a good idea to have high-performance stretch golf carts racing down airport terminals. If you're old or gimpy, you can be rushed to the next gate via these electric carts. Don't feel bad for the guy whose foot just got run over. Now he qualifies for a ride.

Section 2

Making it Through

Chapter 7
High Rise Living

It may seem like a nuisance that the elevator's always broken and your neighbor's new boyfriend is a screamer; but once you get used to it, apartment living isn't really so bad.

Objective 1: Surround Yourself with Good Neighbors

It's important to have good neighbors. In the city, you'll never have the Cleaver's next door; but be sure to avoid winding up in *Melrose Place*.

Method A - Be the least desirable tenant in your building

If nobody wants you as a tenant, you probably have good neighbors. It's better to be the problem than to suffer from one. This method is not recommended for those with low self-esteem.

Method B - Find a building with high vacancy

The black fungus growing on the bathroom ceiling may dissuade others from renting, but the resulting high vacancy rate will reward you with fewer neighbors. No neighbors are good neighbors; and when properly prepared, fungus is a delicacy.

Objective 2: Deal with Noisy Neighbors

If your neighbor is the lead guitarist for a Ramones cover band, a counterattack must be waged.

Method A - Complain to the offender

A simple tap on the door followed by a "Could you please turn the volume down?" won't get you anywhere. Try banging on the door followed by a "If you don't shut the hell up, I'll piss on your doorknob!"

Method B - Out-noise your neighbor

Remarkably, noisy neighbors generally don't like noise if they aren't its source. Noise retaliation is best utilized when the neighbor is sleeping. Weapon of choice: rap music, particularly with bass turned to the highest level. The cold war concept of mutually assured destruction will promote neighborly détente.

Method C - Move

The most effective way to deal with noisy neighbors is to move. In fact, you might want to move to the suburbs where you'll probably have a Hall & Oates cover band next door.

Objective 3: Deal with Quiet, Complaining Neighbors

For those who appreciate a more stimulating environment, you may encounter neighbors who are unappreciative of your taste for auditory pleasure.

Method A - Scare the neighbors into submission

Quiet neighbors are generally easy to intimidate. While entering or exiting your building, be sure to wear your black leather jacket and roll up your sleeve to reveal your skull and crossbones tattoo. No one has to know it's a temporary tattoo that came from your niece's kiddy meal.

Method B - Create an open door policy

If you always welcome your neighbor, a sense of fraternal regard will prevent them from complaining. But when they show up Friday night with Monopoly in tow, don't say you weren't warned.

Objective 4: Cope with Water Leaks

Fans of physics will appreciate a demonstration of gravitational liquid dynamics, but even fans of biology are unlikely to appreciate the aforementioned black fungus that results from a water leak in the apartment upstairs.

Method A - Reside on a high floor

The math is simple; the fewer apartments above you, less is the probability of a leak. Don't mind the higher price of admission or the snobs that live on your floor; these are sacrifices well worth making.

Method B - Think of the flood in your foyer as an opportunity

Wading through two inches of water in your apartment can seem like a downer, but it's really an opportunity to redecorate. After all, did you really want that uninsured oriental silk carpet passed down to you by your favorite grandmother? The factory-made replica is so much easier to maintain.

Method C - Encapsulate your apartment with a non-permeable membrane

While this may appear to be an effective method, it will cause suffocation and hence is not recommended.

Special Section

Apartment Voyeurism

Privacy can be difficult to achieve in an urban environment. One should be aware of the risks and respond accordingly. Please note that the advice given in this special section assumes that the reader is not an exhibitionist or nudist. Exhibitionists should reverse all instructions. Nudists won't have any hang-ups about any of this and can proceed to the next chapter.

PEOPLE CAN SEE YOU

The building across the street is also a high rise. Its residents probably don't want to see you in the buff so pretend you have company and put your pants back on.

JUST BECAUSE YOU CAN'T SEE THEM DOESN'T MEAN THEY CAN'T SEE YOU

Imagine walking around naked in total comfort with the blinds open slightly to bring in the light. No one can see you because there aren't any persons visible to you, right? Wrong. Bend over and position your eyes where your privates were moments ago and check the real status of your presumed stealth. If you see fourteen people across the street laughing, you've miscalculated.

DON'T FORGET ABOUT WINDOW WASHERS

They come from nowhere and always at your most personal moments. Ropes swinging in front of your window are the surest sign that a window washer will be coming soon to peer in at you. Anytime you see the hint of a rope, close the shades.

Chapter 8
Elevators

Elevators are a frequent complaint of the urban experience. However, when you think about it, it's pretty cool that you're hurtling through a shaft in a 4,000 pound metal box at 60 mph.

Objective 1: Prevent Others from Catching an Elevator

Elevator etiquette clearly states that the moment elevator doors begin to close, no one else may enter. But it seems there's always someone who didn't read today's *Miss Manners*.

Method A - Pretend to hold the "Open Door" button while pushing the "Close Door" button

When using this method, casually acknowledge the presence of the person trying to catch the elevator, using body language to imply you'll hold the door. Immediately press the "Close Door" button and show an expression of surprise as the elevator departs without them. This method often fails because "Close Door" buttons on elevators are not connected to anything.

Method B - Pretend to look unsuccessfully for the "Open Door" button

The author's personal favorite, this method makes one appear friendly when, in fact, you are looking right at the "Open Door" button and have no intention of using it.

Method C - Shout "Back Off!"

This method will generally stun the person(s) attempting to catch the elevator, stopping them in their tracks. It will also provide you additional space as others on the elevator will cower in the farthest corner.

Objective 2: Prevent Others from Holding the Door Open

You shouldn't feel guilty for wanting to hurt the person who held the door open in order to squeeze in an additional four people. But as members of a peace-loving society, other alternatives are available.

Method A - *Scowl at the passenger who reaches for the "Open Door" button*

If you want to stop someone from pushing the "Open Door" button, you'll need a particularly nasty scowl. But remember, if you scowl too much, your eyebrows will stick together and become one.

Method B - *Position yourself in front of the elevator panel*

Position yourself in a manner that will require anyone else to enter your personal space to reach the elevator panel. The rarity of people who are comfortable infringing on personal space prevents most from pushing the "Open Door" button. This method will not work with modern elevators that have two elevator panels.

Method C - *Slap the person's hand prior to it reaching the "Open Door" button*

This method, while effective, may get you arrested. Hence, it is not recommended.

Objective 3: Catch an Elevator

In contrast to preventing others from catching elevators, it's sometimes necessary to catch an elevator at someone else's expense. But out of courtesy, please use these methods sparingly.

Method A - Shout "Hold the Elevator!"

As much as people don't want to hold an elevator, human behavior is such that, when confronted, there is usually at least one person in a group that responds to an order.

Method B - The Umbrella Swipe

When carrying an umbrella, an effective method of catching an elevator is to swipe the umbrella between the closing doors. The doors can be almost closed without risking major injury, except to the umbrella. If one is not carrying an umbrella, other items may be substituted such as briefcases, purses and shopping bags. Always avoid one's arm or other body part from being used accidentally or intentionally within the range of closing doors.

Method C - Sprint full speed toward the closing elevator doors and dive

While extremely dangerous, largely ineffective, and just plain stupid, this method will appeal to helmet-wearing dramatists.

Special Section
Fun on Elevators

Many methods have been developed to improve the pleasure of the elevator experience.

JUMP RIGHT BEFORE AN ASCENDING ELEVATOR ARRIVES AT A FLOOR

One may reach previously unthought of heights if timed properly. Simply wait until the ascending elevator has almost reached its destination, then at the moment the elevator begins to decelerate, leap with all your ability. You will retain the upward momentum of the elevator without losing any of the force of the jump. But don't blame the author when you hit your head on the ceiling or break your legs on the way down.

EXPEL GAS AS YOU LEAVE AN ELEVATOR

There is a certain pleasure in knowing that others will be confined in an area where they have no choice but to inhale the residue of a gaseous release while you simply walk away. The satisfaction is increased by the knowledge that people on the elevator will be wondering which occupant was the perpetrator when, in fact, no one within that group is the guilty party. A word of precaution: it's better to release too late and weaken the impact than it is to release too early and subject yourself to the odor.

Chapter 9
Peace & Quiet

Though the symphonic harmony of horns blaring at 3 a.m. is music to an urbanite's ears, occasionally one needs to stop and hear the Muzak. Not to worry, there are many ways to achieve the peace and quiet you desire.

Objective 1: Experience Serenity

To achieve serenity in the city, you may need more than a warm bath, chamomile tea and Enya mood music.

Method A - Redefine serenity

What is serenity? It's what you want it to be. Can you dig it?

Method B - Get into Yoga

In recent years, self-proclaimed yoga gurus contorting on tropical beaches have given meditation a questionable reputation. However, it turns out bizarre mantras and twisting into a pretzel really can be relaxing. So sign up for yoga at the local park district. And don't worry... if the class is full, Jazzercise has openings next door.

Method C - Engage the services of a mental health professional

If you have difficulty achieving serenity, the problem may not be the world that surrounds you. There's a reason why people refer to your watch as a cuckoo clock.

Objective 2: Discover a Quiet Escape

Quiet in the city is not as hard to find as one may think. Just keep your mind open and your ears closed.

Method A - Go into a highrise stairwell

Protected from extraneous noise, these concrete havens can provide an almost eerie quiet. Unfortunately, in a residential highrise, the quiet may be shattered as the door slams behind the guy two floors up who needs a place to indulge his two-pack-a-day habit. Worse are office building stairwells where you'll find the door has locked behind you and you have to walk down forty floors to get out.

Method B - Insert earplugs

Earplugs have a remarkable ability to prevent noise from reaching your ear drums. Unfortunately, in your bliss of silence, you won't hear the blaring horn of the bus that's about to hit you.

Method C - Live in an apartment on the 52nd floor

While you'll still hear the occasional siren or horn, it will be so muffled, you'll hardly notice. Another perk: you'll get great exercise when the elevator breaks.

Objective 3: Find Isolation

Sometimes you just want to be alone. Don't let the 7 million people in the surrounding 1 mile radius deter you. Solitude is closer than you think.

Method A - Go into a bathroom and lock the door

The bathroom is an ideal place of isolation. Privacy, no windows, and you can see a man about a horse. This method is not recommended if you have three roommates and no other bathrooms.

Method B - Go into a closet and close the door

This method, while somewhat effective, has negative aspects that make it a distant second choice when compared to the bathroom. First, some closets don't have a light so you may be stuck in the dark. Second, you might bump into the ironing board, causing it to hit the toolbox, which will subsequently fall on your foot.

Method C - Move to the country

While isolation from people may be found in the country, you are surrounded by the incessant racket of chirping birds, rustling leaves, and babbling brooks. By the time the crickets start their mating call at dusk, you'll be high-tailing it back to the city.

Chapter 10
Crime

After your sixth bike and ninth car stereo have been stolen, you may think that city life is not for you. However, when something serious occurs, would you rather have city cops respond, or a suburban deputy whose biggest collar in the past twelve months was busting up a teenage party in a cornfield?

Objective 1: Avoid Being the Victim of a Crime

Contrary to popular theory, you can exit a city apartment without being mugged. The difficult task is timing your exit with the scheduled drive-by of area police.

Method A - *Don't provoke altercations with large people carrying weapons*

No matter how mad you are, and for whatever reason, it's not a good idea to provoke someone more physically fit than yourself and/or someone carrying a weapon. Don't get cocky just because you've completed TaeBo Gold.

Method B - *Don't lock your car door*

Car doors should remain unlocked if parking in an unattended area. If someone intends to steal your car, they will. The same applies for your car stereo. If it's the stereo they're after, you may as well not have to replace a broken window, too.

Method C - *Contort your face to appear psychotic*

Criminals are usually reluctant to commit a crime against a psychotic. It's easier to commit a crime against a psychologically sound individual because their reactions are much more predictable. Psychotic facial contortion can be achieved by opening your eyes as wide as possible, raising your left eyebrow (right if you're a lefty), hiding your neck with your chin and covering your teeth with your lips.

Objective 2: Have the Police Diligently Pursue a Crime

Even Sully Baby must admit that this is where urban crime-fighting kind of falls off. While initial response is quick and sufficient, after the immediate threat is gone, it's unlikely a major urban police force will concentrate on the recovery of your $200 bike.

Method A - Demand service

In this method, sternly declare to the officer that his/her sworn duty is to serve and protect. Caution: Stand at least one foot away from the officer while making this demand because the resulting explosion of laughter will cause doughnut chunks to vault a minimum of eight inches from the officer's mouth.

Method B - Offer an incentive compensation package

Offer to deliver two dozen doughnuts and a box of coffee to the precinct upon return of your 10-speed. Not only are you likely to see your bike again, but the arresting officer will be one step closer to Captain. Talk about a win-win situation.

Method C - Become a police officer

Typically, the theft of your two prized garden gnomes are not cause enough for a drastic change in professions. But haven't you been thinking of a career in law enforcement anyway?

Objective 3: Help Eliminate Crime

Nobody likes a whiner. Get off your duff and do something.

Method A - Stop committing crimes

To reduce crime rates, it's essential for you to stop committing crimes. Encourage your friends and neighbors to do the same.

Method B - Become a vigilante

Fans of *Deathwish* may think becoming a vigilante is cool. It's not, unless you want to be arrested. Still, you gotta love Charles Bronson.

Method C - Join community policing efforts

Admit it, you watch *Cops* and *World's Wildest Police Chases*, and you've always wanted to ride shotgun in a squad car. Before long, you'll probably be able to collar a guy for littering.

Chapter 11
Smokers

Although the EPA has imposed laws on every factory in the city, they have yet to regulate the 35 smokers standing below a black cloud in front of your office building. If you've already met your daily recommended allowance of secondhand smoke, you'll have to steer clear.

Objective 1: Avoid Smoke from the Smoker in Front of You

It's quite common to be walking on a sidewalk and become suddenly enveloped in a cloud of cancerous smoke. Odds are it's not from the demolition of the asbestos-filled building you're walking by, but the cigar-smoking schmo five paces ahead of you.

Method A - Walk faster

Given the adverse affect of smoking to the lungs, smokers usually walk slowly and are easy to pass. Pick up your pace and as you pass the offender, ask if they passed the emissions test at their last physical.

Method B - Walk slower

There are times when a smoker is walking rapidly. This typically occurs when the individual has only recently taken up the habit and doesn't yet have the low lung capacity of a veteran smoker. In this case, slow down.

Method C - Bob 'n Weave

Just watch the smoke as it exits the smoker's mouth. If it wafts to the right, bob left; if it wafts left, weave right. You'll look like a fool, but you'll be breathing clean air.

Objective 2: Avoid Smoke as You Walk into a Building

States and municipalities have aggressively pursued a reduction in secondhand smoke over the past decade. Positive results include restaurants where smoked salmon doesn't mean your fish passed by the guy smoking reds, and offices where now the only area you can't breath safely is by "B.O. Bob's" cubicle. Unfortunately, it's now impossible to walk into a building without being engulfed by smoke from those who've been forced onto the streets.

Method A - Hold your breath

A benefit to restricting smoking to a specific area is that one can easily pass by that area while holding one's breath. Simply assess when you are about to be engulfed in smoke, take a deep breath and don't breathe again until you are safely inside.

Method B - Use the side door

For some reason, smokers prefer to puff in high traffic areas such as the front door. Maybe it's the whole "it's a free country" thing. Use the side door and avoid the smoke.

Method C - Crawl into the building

Everyone knows smoke rises, so when you see it coming, stop, drop and crawl. Remember to wear kneepads and don't get your fingers stuck in the revolving door.

Objective 3: Prevent a Smoker from Brushing Their Cigarette Against You

You'd think that someone who wouldn't want to singe their own clothes with a burning stick would understand why a passerby might feel the same way. But that is clearly not the case.

Method A - Stare at the cigarette with a look of determined disgust

This method seems to make sense at first, but cigarettes don't have eyes or personalities. Try staring down the smoker instead.

Method B - Move aside

This is the easy way out and you wouldn't be in the city if you took the easy way out. Go to Method C.

Method C - Loudly proclaim, "You better not touch me with that cigarette or I'll shove it up your ass!"

While this method isn't polite, it is effective. However, the threat to "shove it up your ass" should only be stated proverbially.

Section 3
Having Some Fun

Chapter 12
Restaurants

A dearth of Dairy Queens highlight a severe deficiency in urban cuisine. Although your craving for a Dilly Bar will never be fully satisfied, the city does offer an extraordinary assortment of dining alternatives. And even though Sully Baby is the author of Sully Baby's 100 Day Diet, he knows his way around a restaurant.

Objective 1: Procure Authentic Ethnic Food

So a $42 plate of Asian-Fusion cuisine prepared by a guy who grew up in Berkley doesn't appeal to your palate. The city's melting pot of ethnicity provides a great variety of real ethnic food.

Method A - Look for a menu that you can't read
Don't panic when today's special is lamb eyeballs; you've found an authentic ethnic restaurant. It's always good to try new things... but Sully Baby recommends the Shish-Kabob.

Method B - Eat in ethnic neighborhoods
Logic dictates that in ethnic neighborhoods, you'll find the best and most authentic ethnic foods.

Method C - Diversify the ethnic background of your friends
By diversifying your friends to include many ethnic backgrounds, you'll not only become a more complete human being, but you'll be able to get the names of great ethnic restaurants.

Objective 2: Procure Authentic Junk Food

Fans of deep-fried delicacies will revel in the junk food the city has to offer. While it's easy to get junk food anywhere, authentic junk food is becoming harder to find.

Method A - Go where the rent is cheap

No self-respecting junk food establishment can afford the high-rent district. Cheap prices charged to customers combined with the cost of high quality grease means proprietors have nothing left for rent.

Method B - Look for places where they've done a bad job removing the health department stickers

The best gyros, burgers and hot dogs can only be found in dives where the floor hasn't been cleaned for at least two years and the preparers ignore the sign that says, "Wash your hands after using the bathroom." Don't worry, your clogged arteries will kill you before the bacteria gets a chance.

Objective 3: Avoid Tourist Restaurants

In an unexplained phenomenon, tourists are attracted to restaurants with long lines, high prices, bland food and unacceptable customer service. With a trained eye, these traps can be avoided.

Method A - Stay away from theme restaurants

It's better to experience the event rather than eating beneath the leftover memorabilia.

Method B - Don't go to restaurants that have their own line of apparel

If you find yourself in a restaurant where the gift shop is twice the size of the kitchen, buy a souvenir key chain but find your meal elsewhere.

Method C - Beware of slow-moving, 50,000 pound vehicles

Don't go to a restaurant within 1000 feet of a tour bus with Iowa plates. The quilting club just drove in from their casino field trip. Get out of the way. The slots weren't kind and these ladies are hungry.

Objective 4: Don't Get Financially Hosed

It's just not right to pay $6 for a dinner salad when you can buy a Sully Baby book for a nickel less. Dine wisely and buy more books.

Method A - Go to restaurants with a prix fixe menu

Also known as a value meal, you can't beat a deal where everything's included.

Method B - Don't eat at the hotel's coffee shop

The "9" you see to next to the listing for freshly squeezed orange juice is not referring to ounces. Add toast, tax and tip and you could've put a down payment on a summer house in the country.

Chapter 13
Night Life

So you want a night out on the town, but think the dueling pianos of Elton John and Billy Joel are better locked up in Atlantic City. "Whatarewegonnado?" will no longer be an issue after reading Sully Baby's nightlife advice.

Objective 1: Gain Entrance to the Hottest Club

Once you've found the perfect club, you don't want to be outside the entire night waiting for your turn to enter.

Method A - Grease the guy at the door

The 6'4", 250 pound bouncer isn't looking at you in disgust because he's a pillar of ethics. He just wants twenty bucks instead of the five you just tried to hand him.

Method B - Become famous

Club owners always welcome famous customers. But being a losing contestant on *The Price is Right* in 1983 doesn't qualify.

Method C - Confidently walk to the front of the line

This method is frequently successful as the bouncer may assume you are someone he should know and allow to enter. But be ready to be humiliated when he points to the end of the line.

Objective 2: Select Appropriate Attire

Short of wearing black 24/7, you won't find attire that works for everything.

Method A - Dress formally

Nothing says class like a tux or satin dress. If you're off to the gala benefit for the monkey house at the children's zoo, put on your finest. Unfortunately, nothing screams "no class" more than the way you're dancing and drinking.

Method B - Dress theatrically

Although limited, there are times when an ascot and beret are appropriate attire... like that time you and Sunshine went to the herbal poetry slam.

Method C - Barely dress

For those of you planning to go to the hot new dance club, you'll want suitable attire. Men and women alike will want to wear a sheer top and skin-tight pleather pants.

Objective 3: Don't Go Broke

The city not only offers a plethora of nightlife, but also the opportunity to go broke paying for it. Twenty bucks cover for the luxury to dance in an over-crowded club that charges $10 for a drink will drain resources that could otherwise be used to save for that 33 foot motor home you've always dreamed of owning.

Method A - Get a student ID

Student ID's work wonders, particularly for theatrical events. And you won't be stuck at the local junior high school's rendition of *Our Town*. You'll get into great shows at a reasonable price with a student ID.

Method B - Go to a kegger at your friend's place

Okay, it might not be the swankiest soiree in town, but you can't beat the price of Moose's eviction party. If you want to get that hottie a drink, all you have to do is walk to the bathtub and pull the tap.

Method C - Know the right people

If you know the bouncer at a club, you're getting in free; and if you're buddies with a ticket broker, you'll get a cheap line on great tickets.

Chapter 14
Dating

For anyone who's spotted an eighteen pound rat while taking a romantic gondola ride in Venice, you know urban dating can be tough. But with proper know-how, you can find paradise by the city lights.

Objective 1: Find a Romantic Spot

The city may not have drive-in movie theaters or fields filled with wild flowers, but inspiration point doesn't necessarily refer to a place on the map (if you know what I mean).

Method A - Parks (during daylight)

Parks abound with an aura of romance. It is important to recognize, however, a visit at night by a loving couple is not recommended unless both members are equipped with pepper spray, a loud whistle and a bat. This will put a dent into the romance of all but the most militaristic couples.

Method B - Cafés (particularly at night)

Cafés benefit from a quasi-European, quasi-intellectual, quasi-bohemian flavor, in a setting with undersized tables crammed together. The combined effect is one of romance, at least until the slobbering oaf at the table next to you knocks his chair into your date, causing Campari and soda to spill all over the table.

Method C - Bodies of water

Most cities offer numerous bodies of water which exude romance. Just stay away from paddle boats in city parks, unless you think it's romantic to wait in line with screaming children, sit in a puddle, and set sail in two feet of polluted water.

Objective 2: Move on After a Break-Up

Breaking up is always hard to do, but in the city you have a sea full of fish waiting for you. So cast your line, my friend.

Method A - Go stag

No matter how long your relationship lasted, it's time to take stock of all the city has to offer. Independence is good. Play the field.

Method B - Rebound

For those who aren't interested in playing the field, the city is also filled with people looking for that special someone. Before you go searching, be sure to reference the special section at the end of this chapter.

Method C - Lay in bed depressed

Just because opportunity knocks doesn't mean you have to open the door. Put on your tattered sweat suit, stop taking showers and think of all the people that surround you in the city... yet you have no one.

Objective 3: Go on a Cheap but Satisfying Dinner Date

Food is a primary focus of the urban date. Unfortunately going out to eat can be a financially depleting experience.

Method A - Make dinner at home

By making dinner at home, you're sending a message that you care enough to go through the labor of cooking. The benefit of saving money in the bargain is frosting on the cake. Just don't make a quiche with the six month old eggs sitting in your fridge.

Method B - Go to a neighborhood restaurant

The benefits of going to a neighborhood restaurant are infinite. Among the benefits: reduced waiting times, cheaper prices, good food and good service. In addition, you'll be viewed by your date as more interesting than someone who goes standard issue. And to think you were just trying to save cab fare.

Method C - Go to restaurants without a liquor license

The most expensive part of a dinner date is often the liquor consumed. Go to a restaurant without a liquor license and you'll reduce the bill dramatically. If your date questions your choice, reply with "I'm recovering."

Special Section

Where Not To Meet People

10 CENT WING NITE

LAUNDROMATS

STREET CORNERS

MARTINI BARS

DOUGHNUT SHOPS AT 3AM

BIRTHING CLASS

LAS VEGAS

PUBLIC TRANSIT

PIER 42

CROSBY STILLS NASH & YOUNG REUNION TOUR

Chapter 15
Movie Theaters

Just because it costs $150 to take your family of four to a downtown movie doesn't mean Lurch won't take the seat in front of you. Extreme measures should be taken to ensure a satisfactory urban theater experience.

Objective 1: Spend Less Than $25 per Person Going to the Movies

A $14 ticket is only the beginning; add $7 for popcorn, $6 for a soda, and $30 for parking and you've got a serious cash flow crunch.

Method A - Go to a matinee

It's too bad that you have nothing better to do than go to a matinee on a beautiful day, but at least you'll save some money and be on time for your 4:00 Scrabble tourney.

Method B - Say you're a senior citizen

The American Association of Retired Persons has influence second only to the National Rifle Association. Wielding their power from Congress to the Hollidome, seniors get discounts almost everywhere. Hunch over, whip out the walker and put mothballs in your pockets. The sixteen year old selling tickets will believe you're sixty-five.

Method C - Sneak in food and beverages

There is actually one redeeming quality of the hip-hop baggy pants fashion craze. You can crotch a bag of chips and a six-pack of cola with no one noticing. Your consumption binge will cost less than a small box of Goobers purchased at the theater.

Objective 2: Have an Empty Seat in Front of You

The most frustrating experience of movie-going is not being able to get a good look at the movie because of the gigantic head obstructing your view.

Method A - Cough profusely
The ideal method to get a clear view of the movie is threatening the area with an unknown, but clearly detrimental, health condition. Start coughing before the movie starts. If you are accompanied by a friend, take turns coughing and bring cough drops. They'll soothe your throat and the scent will add credibility to your condition.

Method B - Speak loudly
If you and your friend banter loudly before the show, other theater-goers will stay away. If you're alone, yell at the screen and even fewer will dare to approach.

Method C - Breathe on the offender
There are times when a patron is so self-absorbed that they will not notice your coughing fits or irritating voice, and proceed to sit in front of you. Blow fine but firm directed breath on the back of the offender's neck. The person is likely to move his/her seat because of the almost unbearable irritation which it causes.

Objective 3: Stop Someone from Talking

One of the rudest things a human being can do is talk during a movie. People who do so are inconsiderate, narcissistic and unaware of appropriate social behavior.

Method A - *Politely request the offender(s) to be quiet*

If the offender is very large and you fear physical repercussions, this is the method of choice. Just don't be upset when it doesn't work.

Method B - *Throw soft candy at the offender*

Soft mints are the weapon of choice for movie theater warfare. The chocolate shell embraces the minty mass until it explodes on impact. Only use fresh soft mints.

Method C - *"Spray Attack"*

In a situation when virtually everyone in the theater is talking, certain individuals choose to "spray attack." A spray attack is when one takes a boxful of popcorn and flings the entire contents into the air, showering kernels over the perps. Spray attackers should be prepared to immediately depart the premises.

Method D - *Loudly proclaim, "Shut the hell up!"*

This is, hands down, the most effective method for mitigating speaking during a movie. It's forceful and unpredictable. When caught off-guard, people tend to obey.

Chapter 16
The Beach

Clenching your butt cheeks may not make you look any better while sporting your Speedo, but you can have fun at the beach anyway.

Objective 1: Get a Tan

You may think the red of your nipples complements your milky white skin, but no one else does. Time to get a tan, and while you're at it, shave the hair off your back. That goes for you too, missy.

Method A - Lie in the sun

Lying in the sun requires time and effort, often provides unacceptable results, and is dangerous to your health. It's okay to expose your body, just keep it away from the sun.

Method B - Go to a tanning booth

Who needs the sun for beautifully bronzed skin? Tanning spas are convenient and reasonably priced. Don't worry about germs left behind from the last guy. Watered-down glass cleaner is known to kill at least 30% of bacteria.

Method C - Apply tanning cream to yourself (or have another do it; always more enjoyable)

While they're artificial, tanning creams provide the look of a nice even tan with little effort and minimal risk. Applied in minutes without exposure to the sun's rays, this is the optimal method for achieving a tan. As an added benefit, your bright orange skin will reduce the probability of being the victim of a hunting accident.

Objective 2: Avoid Crowds

One of the most disturbing aspects of going to an urban beach is sharing a quarter acre plot of sand with 500,000 people.

Method A - Go early

One of the few times a beach is not crowded is in the morning. The beach is beautiful at dawn; the sun casting its warm glow, only hinting that it will soon scald the earth with its nuclear inferno.

Method B - Go late

While going to a beach late in the afternoon has the benefit of avoiding crowds, beware: the crowd is gone but their garbage is not.

Method C - Make yourself a nuisance

If you must go to the beach at peak time, you'll need to clear a crowd. Yes, you too can be the family that yells, lets their two year old urinate on the beach, and turns the volume up on their boom box. Find the best location at the beach, squeeze your blanket into an impossibly small area of sand, start role playing, and watch the crowd around you flee.

Objective 3: Take a Dip in the Water

The glistening water beckons. But beware: the shimmer is the sun reflecting off radiator fluid pouring from a waste pipe two blocks away.

Method A - Take a side trip to your friend's place, you know, the one with the rooftop swimming pool

It's always better to take a dip in clean water. Very few people urinate in private pools because there's almost always a clean bathroom nearby. At a public beach the choice is more frequently "dip and release."

Method B - Pour a gallon of water over your head

Bring a container from home and fill up at the water fountain. Pour the water over your head, close your eyes, and pretend you're swimming. For waders, follow the same procedure but only pour the water over your legs.

Method C - Go swimming

If you're a risk taker, you might want to jump right into the muck. Check your health insurance coverage for exclusions beforehand.

Special Section

Observe & Critique Others at the Beach

Urban beaches offer an endless parade of people in attire that is more revealing than the undergarments regularly worn by these same individuals. In fact, one of the principle functions of the beach is to provide a culturally acceptable vehicle for exhibitionism and voyeurism. After all, isn't that why you go to the beach?

POSITION YOURSELF FOR OPTIMAL VIEWING

For best sight-seeing, one should seek a bird's-eye view and high traffic flow. Bring your binoculars and remember, high traffic flow is best found near food vendors and restrooms.

BE CRITICAL

As long as you're rude enough to comment on people's appearances, you might as well slam them. It's easier and more fun to criticize than to compliment.

FORGET ABOUT THE WAY YOU LOOK

Yes, there will be people being critical of the way you look, returning the favor which you have just paid to them, but why worry? You're looking hot, smokin' hot.

The End

About the Author

Does it really matter?